TEEN LIFE™

FREQUENTLY ASKED QUESTIONS ABOUT

Online Gaming
Addiction

Holly
Cefrey

J
616.85
Cef

ROSEN
PUBLISHING®

New York

For the gamers

Published in 2010 by The Rosen Publishing Group, Inc.
29 East 21st Street, New York, NY 10010

First Edition

Library of Congress Cataloging-in-Publication Data

Cefrey, Holly.
Frequently asked questions about online gaming addiction /
Holly Cefrey.
    p. cm.—(FAQ: teen life)
Includes index.
ISBN 978-1-4358-3548-1 (library binding)
1. Internet addiction. 2. Internet games—Social aspects. 3.
Impulse control disorders. 4. Compulsive behavior. I. Title.
RC569.5.I54C44 2010
616.85'84—dc22

        2009015476

Manufactured in Malaysia

CPSIA Compliance Information: Batch #TWW10YA: For Further Information contact Rosen Publishing, New York, New York at 1-800-237-9932

Contents

WHAT IS ONLINE GAMING ADDICTION?

The Internet opens up a whole other world, one in which most of us could spend hours and hours visiting, weekly and daily. The Internet gives us access to networks that provide services such as e-mail, chat rooms, and the Web. According to the Pew Research Center, nearly 87 percent of youths use the Web, and 51 percent of these surfers do so daily. Youths spend their time checking e-mail, Web surfing, shopping, and visiting chat rooms. They use the Web for studying and researching, both for educational and personal reasons. Youths also use the Web for games. Online gaming is incredibly popular. According to the MacArthur Foundation, 97 percent of American youths (ages twelve to seventeen) play video games.

"Online gaming" is a general term for a number of ways in which a person can "game" while using the Web.

Gaming can be single player, where an individual Web surfer plays alone. Gaming can also be multiplayer. This is where a surfer and other players are able to enjoy playing a game together. Multiplayer games can be accessed on the Web and through gaming systems that connect through the Web.

Online Games Through Web Sites

A surfer can simply visit a Web site that has gaming applications on it. A basic version of this type of online game is when a surfer takes part in quizzes at a Web site. This is a single player type of game. Many of these games are playable by using just the mouse or keyboard. Keys on the keyboards, like the space bar and the arrow keys, allow for movement or action. Many educational and museum-based Web sites offer these games.

The surfer answers the questions or carries out the activities, and the gaming application keeps track of a score. The player's score will indicate a level of knowledge. Results may be compared to those of the other surfers who have visited the site. The score may have further directions, such as where else to look for information in order to learn more. It is a fun way to spend time, and the player learns something at the same time.

An example of this is the Smithsonian's *Digging for Answers* game, where the player gets to choose from a variety of topics. Basic knowledge is quizzed. When an answer is incorrect, a tip box pops up and provides links to where the player can find the correct answer. Surfers may find that minutes can turn into hours

The Web is a place that brings people together in search of knowledge, answers, and fun. Online knowledge and memory games are a great way to enjoy learning with others.

while playing these types of games. As long as learning is taking place, this can be time well spent.

Many games can be accessed through online game companies. Many of these companies offer free games on their Web sites. The companies make money by selling advertisements. Other companies pay the game company to put ads on the Web site so that they can reach surfers. Some of these game companies will ask surfers to join clubs or submit information before allowing them to use the free games. This information may be as simple as creating a username and password. Some may also ask for the surfer's e-mail address. Some of these companies may make money off of collecting e-mail addresses or other personal information. They sell the addresses to advertisers or other companies.

It is important to read the privacy policy, terms of use, and agreements that are part of signing up for anything online. Most registrations will have a box that the surfer must click to show that he or she has read the policy or agreement. When a surfer clicks "yes," it means that he or she agrees to everything within the agreement. This may include giving permission to share the surfer's e-mail address with other companies. When a site offers games for free, it is really important to make sure that they are really offering them for free. Some sites claim they offer free games, but the surfer is taken to screens that request payment to play further or play full versions of the game.

Some companies make surfers pay for membership fees, or they charge money to play or download the games. In this case, the surfer takes the gaming application from the Web site and puts it on his or her computer. Many games can be downloaded for free instead of for payment. It is just a matter of searching for the companies that truly offer free games and downloads. A surfer should not spend a lot of money on games when so many free ones are available. Spending a lot of money on games can mean that the surfer puts too much focus on gaming. When a surfer has more games than he or she can even play, it is time to stop buying or downloading and consider if it is too much.

Games found at gaming sites include racing, shooting, role-playing, classic arcade, adventure, and memory games. Memory games test the surfer's memory by quickly showing the surfer something, then asking him or her to remember it. Classic arcade games are games that were played when computer games were first introduced to the public. *PONG* and *Pac-Man* are classic arcade games.

Adventure, shooting, role-playing, and racing games are an easy way to spend several hours online. The desire to get to the next level can be very strong. Each time a level is finished, the surfer has a sense of accomplishment or of doing something correctly. The surfer may also be trying to beat his or her own best score or the scores of others.

This feeling of accomplishment can become addictive. The gamer seeks this activity above many other things. When a gamer wants to play video games rather than do important things, like seeing friends, eating dinner, or getting fresh air and exercise, he or she may be addicted.

Home Gaming Is Not Solo

Video games are fun, and anything fun is something we like to do again and again. While many people may think that video games take youths away from activities and making friends, they may be wrong. According to the study "Teens, Video Games, and Civics" by the Pew Research Center, video gaming is not for loners. Only 24 percent of gamers ages twelve to seventeen prefer to play alone. The remaining gamers will play alone sometimes but also play with others regularly. This means that games are a social activity for most gamers. They are

Classic arcade games like *Pac-Man*, as seen here, are still fun to play. While the graphics may be simple, gamers are still drawn to the challenges and try to claim the highest score.

an activity where people can share with each other and interact or communicate with each other.

As a social activity, a person tries to share the experience with others, instead of withdraw, or no longer take part in something. When a person is withdrawn, he or she is not friendly or sociable. The person may be very quiet and isolated from others. The 24 percent of gamers who only play alone will hopefully have other favorite activities. These activities may include sports, exercise, recreational reading, arts and crafts, or hobbies. If they spend most of their time gaming alone, this can lead to

Internet cafes often allow gamers to play with or next to each other. Here, a gamer shows that his role-playing game is over because his character was killed.

being withdrawn. It is also a sign that the gamer spends way too much time gaming. Having a variety of activities, even if done alone, is a healthier lifestyle than focusing on a single activity like gaming.

According to the Pew study, about 73 percent of youths play video games on a laptop or desktop computer. About 86 percent also use home gaming systems such as Xbox, Wii, or PlayStation. Home gaming systems are also Internet and Web-capable, allowing more than one player to play a game, even if that player is not in the same room.

According to the study, 27 percent of gamers play with other people through the Internet. This allows a connection between players, creating yet another great world to dive into, where gamers feel a sense of friendship and belonging. Gamers understand each other; they share the same interests. When a gamer's only friends are those that he or she has met or found online, it's time for the gamer to reevaluate this and participate in other activities. Interaction in person with friends and family is important for our emotional development and well-being. A variety of friends with varied interests adds to a person's overall growth and intelligence.

chapter two

HOW DANGEROUS IS IT?

Video games and online gaming are controversial. Some people believe that video games can cause serious addiction. There is a current—and popular—belief that gamers grow dependent on gaming for happiness.

No one needs to play games, but gaming can give us a break from reality. Sometimes, we all need a break. Surfers seek a break where they can forget their worries. Gaming is a perfect pastime for this. It allows us to be challenged, focused, and striving for something that gives us happiness. Some gamers can't wait to play and take every chance they can to get away from it all and disappear into the game.

Game system and online role-playing games are appealing to youths who want to escape. Role-playing games create an alter ego or character for the gamer.

This is known as an avatar. Avatars are the gamers, but they aren't. They're the gamers' version of themselves for the game world. Avatars allow the gamers to do things they can't do in real life. The real world may not be a safe, comfortable, happy, or healthy place for many gamers. They may be picked on at school or be unpopular. They may be shy or clumsy or unskilled at sports. They may have a family life that is full of drama, anger, or trouble. While playing, gamers can be a different character entirely, such as an outgoing hero or a graceful, skilled, or strong athlete. Gamers can be whomever they want to be and create whatever world they want. They can find other "characters" who become guides, teachers, or friends. This creates relationships in the fantasy realm that are just as appealing as those in real life. Sometimes, the fantasy world of gaming can become more appealing than the real world.

This appeal has given rise to a multiplayer environment known as MMORPG. This stands for "massively multiplayer online role-playing game." The game *World of Warcraft* by Blizzard Entertainment is an MMORPG. The company hosts the "worlds" in which the characters live. They have launched these worlds all over the globe. Players first buy the software application or game package. They then pay a fee to play regularly as subscribers. They become subscribers by buying time cards or paying with a credit card.

In December 2008, Blizzard Entertainment announced that it had more than 11.5 million subscribers. This means that a character could wander around in a world and meet countless other subscribers as avatars.

The release of the *World of Warcraft: Wrath of the Lich King* role-playing game was so eagerly awaited, gamers camped outside of retail stores to be among the first to buy it.

A variety of MMORPGs offer choices for how subscribers can play. They can play against each other, or they can play against the environment. This is PVP (player versus player) and PVE (player versus environment). Players can decide if they're going to be battling other players or joining forces.

Blizzard Entertainment has rules that subscribers must follow. It even posts rules of etiquette. "Etiquette" is how to properly behave toward others. The rules of etiquette for the virtual realm are similar to real-world rules. Relationships between characters can last for days, week, months, or even years. Online weddings between characters have even occurred.

Where People Look for Home

Getting lost in a game is not a bad thing, but getting lost for too long is. The worlds that gamers build online, whether single-player or multiplayer, are not real. They may seem real, but they aren't. The hours spent playing the game cannot replace the hours lost in the real world. The worries, troubles, and problems that were there when the game started are there when it ends. While the game may help relieve stress, stress returns after the game ends. While playing with others online may relieve loneliness, it returns, too. The friendship isn't based on trust, shared experiences, and common likes and dislikes. It's only built on the game. Friendships have to grow through a number of different experiences, not just one shared interest.

The only way to fix the urge to escape is to face what's wrong in life. School and community counselors, teachers, and

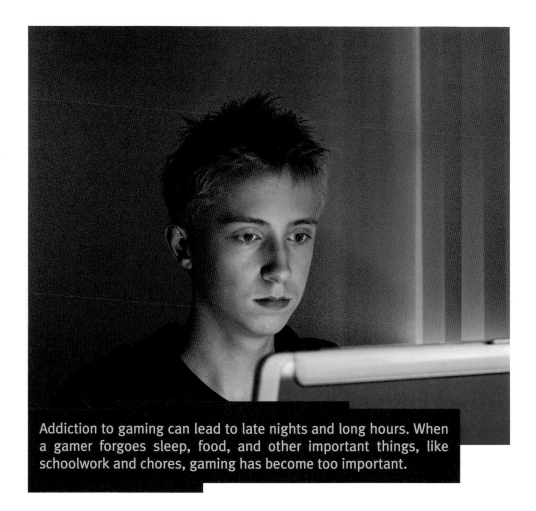

Addiction to gaming can lead to late nights and long hours. When a gamer forgoes sleep, food, and other important things, like schoolwork and chores, gaming has become too important.

religious leaders are excellent resources. They have given advice to hundreds and sometimes thousands of people. An unhappy school, home, and social life are not new things. These teachers and mentors will help gamers face their problems. The game shouldn't be the answer to any problem. It should be something done on occasion for pure enjoyment, not be an escape for hours on end.

There are many books, journals, and articles that will help a gamer better understand his or her personal issues. If an issue is too personal for the library, there are online organizations for almost every issue. A quick Internet search about the particular issue and the word "organization" or "help" will pull up a lot of resources.

Getting in the Game

If gamers are at school, at work, or with family and all they can think about is the game, there may a problem. This is a sign of addiction. Sometimes, gamers obsess about a level that they can't get past. They may use time away from the game to plot how to win the game. When all this thinking takes the place of learning in school or enjoying the company of a friend, gamers need to reevaluate things. If they would rather play the game than enjoy everyday things such as a healthy, well-cooked meal, there may be a problem. If they get grouchy if something else prevents gaming, this can be a sign of addiction. School grades, work performance, and relationships can suffer when one is too focused on gaming. Gamers need to be able to shift their thinking about the game during real life. Otherwise, they are developing an addiction.

Anytime gamers are upset that they're not gaming, they need to take a break and think about why gaming is so important. Why is it more important to game right now, rather than finish homework? Why is it necessary to game right now, when friends want to go outside and have fun? The game will

Standard board games are still a great way to pass the time, and they allow the eyes, mind, and body a much-needed break from intense video gaming.

still be there, now and later. There is no reason to get upset, angry, or withdrawn because the game can't be played for some reason. If this is how gamers feel when they are denied gaming, it's time to take a closer look at themselves and add some other activities to their life.

A healthier way to game is to treat it like a reward. The gamer needs to view the game as the reward for facing challenges or for accomplishing other things first. Finishing a book report early would deserve some solid gaming time. Helping a friend finish a project would deserve some game time. Spending

time with a younger sibling—which can be really challenging—
is worth something, too. All of these things should actually be
rewarding in and of themselves. Doing these things helps a
person grow mentally and spiritually, but addicted gamers
often stop doing these things. They forget about doing large
and small things. They become wrapped up in the game. Using
gaming as a reward for even simple accomplishments can
make it a healthier pastime.

Gamers should be able to put aside the game to do things
and then game freely, either as a reward or for enjoyment. They
should be able to stop gaming for any reason. Addicts often snap
angrily at others when they're asked to quit their activity. They
can become sarcastic or unloving if someone threatens to take
away their game. They begin to plead and promise to do things
so that they can keep playing. When they experience technical
problems, they may break or throw things. They may yell at the
computer or a pet or anything that is nearby.

Gamers can get depressed when they're not gaming.
Sometimes, the depression can be so strong that they
won't do anything else. In order to motivate them, the game
might be offered. Addicts will instantly perk up and do whatever is needed of them so that they can get back to the game.
These mood swings, anger fits, and emotions are all signs of
addiction. Addicted gamers need to take a moment and think
about it. They need to ask themselves, "Why am I getting so
upset? When is the last time I was this upset? What was it
about? How did I cope? Why am I so upset about a simple
game? Why does it mean this much to me?" Taking a moment

to reflect is important. Thinking about things can give a person power to change things.

Lying is another sign of trouble. We often lie to hide a truth that can be disappointing to others. Lying about the time spent gaming is common with addicts. They know they spend too much time doing it, but they hide it so that they can keep doing it. They may lie about finishing other things so that gaming won't be interrupted. They may feel guilty about lying. As more lies are told, gamers will withdraw from their friends, family, and responsibilities. Soon, they are caught in an addictive cycle where the only happiness they have is when gaming.

Myths and Facts

Myth

Online gaming is totally safe from hackers.

Fact: ➡ Even with very careful security, online game companies can be hacked. Credit card numbers, addresses, and other personal information can be stolen. Even Blizzard Entertainment's *World of Warcraft* system has experienced hacks—and still does. Hackers can send e-mails that look like they're from a gaming company. The e-mails may promise free features or upgrades. They ask for usernames and passwords. When gamers give this information, it allows hackers to get to billing and payment information from the real company.

Some sites that look official may offer downloads to improve game play. These files may contain trojans. A trojan is an application or program that looks useful, but in reality it causes harm. Trojans are used to steal account and payment information. Online games and worlds have credits that are worth real money or online services. Hackers also steal these. Nothing online is 100 percent safe, especially in gaming.

Online gaming is safe from predators.

Fact: ●→ Gamers can be hobbyists, they can be predators, and they can be one and the same. Older adults who seek the company of underage persons know where to find them. This includes the gaming world. They seek kids for illegal and inappropriate activities. They disguise themselves as peers of the same age or close in age. They talk like friends, and they act like friends. They know how to become important to the online target. They lure targets into virtual relationships that can end in tragedy in the real world.

According to *USA Today*, predators are seeking the game environment because the Federal Bureau of Investigation (FBI) and law enforcement are watching everything else. They purchase game consoles, create avatars, and look for targets. If an avatar is seeking out a player in the game, saying inappropriate things, or trying to get personal information, the gamer needs to block that player through the game system. If parental controls or blocks don't come with the game, contact the game company.

Chatting in an online game is safe, especially with a friend or guardian.

Fact: ➥ Online friends are just that. They need to stay that way. A gamer may be glad for "friendship" as well, but keeping it in the game is safer. When gamers and their real-world friends play, it's important to keep personal information hidden. Chats should only be about the game, and conversation should be between avatars, not friends. Chats between two long-term pals can reveal too much to online friends. Chatting during a game can seem casual, but it can give predators information that they shouldn't have. Some predators will lurk in the background. They may disguise their voice to be that of a young girl or boy. They'll take part in chats and steer conversations toward releasing information. Once a gamer shares a full name, the predator can search for the gamer's location. Even a telephone number allows a trace. The predator will eventually seek a meeting in person, or create one of his or her own.

WHAT ARE THE SIGNS OF GAMING ADDICTION?

One of the strongest signs of addiction is the need to experience something more and more each time. The body and mind get used to an activity, for instance, so we need increases of that activity in order to feel the same excitement. Video games are tricky. Players naturally want to play more as they gain skills. This is because they can go further in the game as skills develop. Wanting to play more of a game may just be a natural part of the experience. Games, in general, since they are for amusement, call us back to them. Think of a board game or a trivia game. The more each is played, the better the player becomes. Of course, that player will grab that game when it's time to play. It is the combination of wanting to game more and more with other signs that will truly indicate if an online gaming addiction is at hand.

Gaming is great, but it cannot beat what exercise and fresh air can do for a person. Everyone should enhance their own lives by participating in physical activities.

As the Web has multiple uses, it's important to think about how much time is spent on it. How much time is spent per day checking e-mail? How much time is spent shopping? How much time is spent surfing for no reason? How much time is spent looking for new games? How much time is spent playing or trying new games? How much time is spent playing favorite games? A person could easily be addicted to the Internet, let alone online games. If a good part of the day or night is spent online, a closer look at habits is necessary.

If your routine is to go from school to the computer to bed, it's probably an addiction. No one needs to be online for that long. Being online that long can lead to real problems, with the mind and body and in relationships. One to two hours after school and a little bit more on the weekend is way healthier than entire blocks of time.

Free time is not meant for one activity. It's meant for many. Free time should be used to take care of anything that remains outside of homework, a job, or household duties. Some of this time should be spent being active. Physical exercise is important for well-being and excellent health. Sitting in front of a game, even if it's a virtual game, does not count as exercise. Playing tennis on a Nintendo Wii doesn't count as exercise either, even though the game requires physical motion. Gamers won't be pushing themselves anywhere near the real limit of live sports.

Bodily Signs of Addiction

The human body is meant to be active, both mentally and physically. Gamers are active, but they repeat the same movements,

Laptops make our lives easier, but they also lead to bad habits. Hours of video gaming can ruin the posture, muscle-tone, and general health of a gamer.

which ultimately leads to limited physical activity. This can cause physical problems if gaming is being done too frequently. The body of a game addict actually shows signs of addiction, such as weight loss.

According to the Nemours Foundation, one out of every three youths is now considered overweight or obese. The foundation claims that youths are spending much less time exercising and much more time in front of the computer. Many addicted gamers will gain weight if they do not balance game time with physical activities. Physical activities will burn off the fat that gaming cannot. Some gamers lose weight because they

Gamers often don't realize that staring at the screen for hours can cause eyestrain, headaches, and sore neck and back muscles. These can lead to long-term health problems, too.

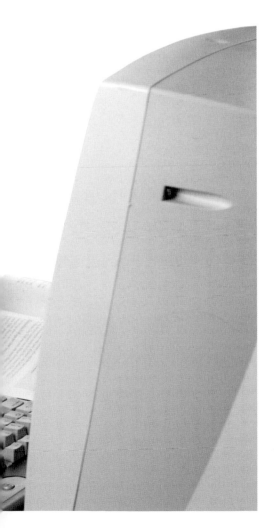

go from eating balanced meals to eating on the run. They eat only when they absolutely have to, so as not to be taken away from the game too long. Some gamers lose their muscle mass because they stop exercising outside of the few things they do while gaming.

There are countless stories of athletic young people who get into gaming for fun, become addicted, and lose their skills and physique gotten from real-world sports. All that time spent gaming can take a true athlete and turn his or her body soft. It's important that for every hour spent sitting during a game, a five- to ten-minute break is taken. During this break, the gamer should get up, stretch, and walk around. He or she could do a few jumping jacks or other exercises. The gamer could do something else, like clean up the room or fold and put away some clothes. This allows blood to flow and muscles to get moving.

When playing virtual sports, it's still necessary to take a break. This is because virtual sports often cause the gamer to repeat a movement. This doesn't work the entire body. It just works the muscles and joints that are being moved in the repeated motion. Overworking these joints without a break can cause strain.

The body shows signs of gaming addiction in the eyes, back, neck, and arms, too. Eyestrain is common from overuse. Staring intently at the bright or dark screen causes fatigue or tiredness. Dry eyes can also be a sign. This is because while staring, we stop blinking. So the eyes are not lubricated or moist like they should be. Gamers need to take a quick break from the screen every ten or twenty minutes. The gamer should take a moment to look at a blank wall 10 or 20 feet (3 to 6 meters) away. He or she should close the eyelids and roll the eyeballs around, up and down, and side to side. Then the gamer should open the eyelids very widely and close them tightly. This will provide a necessary and healthy break for the eyes.

Aches, Syndromes, and Sleep

Addicted gamers often suffer from headaches, backaches, and neckaches. Headaches can range from mild to migraines. The neck and back may be sore from constant strain. Long-term computer users in general often suffer from neck pain. Addicted gamers put stress on their necks and backs through long hours of play. Stretching will help increase blood flow to the back and neck muscles. The real answer, however, is to cut back on hours of gaming. The body is telling the gamer it's not happy for a reason.

According to McLean Psychiatric Hospital, another sign of gaming addiction is carpal tunnel syndrome. Carpal tunnel syndrome takes place in the wrist of the gamer. It is caused by repeated pressure on a nerve in the wrist. It can cause pain to travel through the hand, arm, and shoulder. The condition can also cause numbness and weakness in the hands. It can cause a gamer to lose his or her grip. The gamer will not only have trouble with the joystick or mouse. The difficulty continues when he or she is not gaming. Sufferers often drop objects due to weakness.

The hospital also states that addicted gamers often have sleep problems. Their normal sleep cycles are thrown off by the activity. This leads to another symptom of online gaming addiction: tiredness. Gamers who are tired at school and throughout the day and evening should be concerned. There is currently not enough research on what addicted gaming does to the brain. Like the body, the brain needs a break, too. Gamers should rest their minds and allow for other things to be as important to them as gaming.

Ten Great Questions to Ask a Therapist

1 How much online gaming a day is too much?

2 What online games do you approve of?

3 What kind of online games are best for me to play?

4 Are there any safe gaming groups I could join?

5 Who is safe to talk to online?

6 What can I do to easily quit when I need to?

7 How do I get my brother/sister/friend to stop gaming?

8 How do I decrease my gaming but still have fun?

9 How do I get my old friends back?

10 Can I cure my addiction but still play online games?

HOW CAN I KEEP GAMING UNDER CONTROL?

Sometimes, it is hard to see the obvious. Some signs of addiction may be clear. Some may not be. Being sleepy in school may feel normal after awhile, so when grades start to slip, gaming is not blamed.

Sometimes, it takes friends or family to wake a person up to the truth. Friends and family will notice a very obvious sign of deep gaming addiction. Online gaming addicts neglect or ignore their appearance. They stop caring about personal hygiene. Addicted gamers will stop doing the things that everyone else does as a part of normal hygiene. Addicted gamers often game for hours and days at a time. They may wear the same clothes two or more days in a row. They may go without showering or combing their hair. They may stop brushing their teeth or using deodorant. If friends and family start making comments, it's time to pay attention. If a friend is letting his or her personal hygiene suffer because of gaming, it's time to say something.

Online gaming addicts also give up very important hobbies. This can be shocking to friends and family members. Gamers may love the piano and play it like a professional. Gamers may love football and be the star wide receiver. Gamers might be the art club president or a student leader. When all of these hobbies and talents start becoming less important than gaming, it's time to do something about it. When gamers stop taking music lessons, stop going to sports practice, or stop taking part in extracurricular activities, it is an addiction that needs to be corrected.

Gamers will often make excuses for missing extracurricular activities because they're spiraling into dependency on gaming. The simple answer of "I am just not into it anymore" is not enough. A friend who notices this needs to explain what is happening to the gamer's parent or guardian. The gamer needs to be shown that he or she is obsessed or consumed by the activity. This may be one of the hardest things that a friend or family member can do, but it's important to do something. The sooner a gamer is shown that there is a problem, the easier the recovery may be.

At this point, the gamer needs to be challenged. He or she should be asked to game only one hour a day or less. If he or she cannot do this, it's a clear-cut case of addiction. A friend can challenge a gamer to cut back, but a guardian can actually enforce it. If the gamer can't limit himself or herself to an hour

This mother of a gamer who lost control looks at the On-Line Gamers Anonymous Web site (http://www.olganon.org).

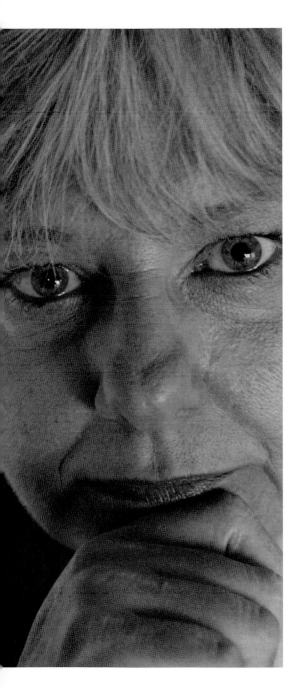

a day—even though the cutback is temporary—it's time to seek real help for addiction.

Losing Is Not Fun, in Games and Life

When family and friends start to talk to the addict, a common response will be denial. The gamer doesn't want to hear that he or she has a problem. The idea of stopping the game seems crazy or silly to the gamer. A friend who keeps calling to say he doesn't see the gamer anymore is just being annoying. A younger sibling who whines that she never gets to play the game is just jealous. A mother or father who nags must have had a bad day and is taking it out on the gamer. The gamer tells himself or herself all of these things. Gamers believe they are the reasons why gaming isn't the problem, everyone else is.

When gaming is so important that a player doesn't feel like social-izing, it's time to rethink how time is spent. It's time to seek the company of real-world friends and do real-world activities.

Gamers will become closer to their friends who are gamers. They'll stop socializing with friends who don't game. They won't think of it as losing friends; they'll just feel like they cleared the way to having more fun. Online, there will be other gamers who are going through a similar situation. The gamer will bond with others who feel like their friends and family "just don't get it."

While gamers may be making virtual friends, they are losing close friends. Virtual friends can't help with problems in the real world. They cannot be there during hard times or moments when a friend close by is really needed. Gamers might even drive friends away without knowing it. They may become so obsessed that their conversations are only about gaming. Some friends just don't want to stick around for it if they're not into gaming. Sometimes, it's too late to bring back old friendships, but people who care are worth trying to regain. Sometimes, it just seems easier to the addict to let friends go and make new friends online.

Doing Something About It

In 2007, Chinese lawmakers announced to the government and public that online gaming addiction is real and dangerous. According to the British Broadcast Corporation (BBC), the Chinese government will enforce regulations or rules for online gaming time. Game makers will be forced to create games that stop after three hours of play. This will make the player get up and take a break. Hopes are that the gamer will

Sometimes, it's easier to understand problems by writing about them. Gamers should chart out how much of their time is spent gaming and list their other activities.

go back to real life. After five hours, the game will shut off entirely. For role-playing games, another idea is that after three hours, the avatar will lose power. After five hours, the avatar will become so challenged that the player will quit playing out of boredom.

If a friend says that he or she thinks you or someone else is gaming too much, listen. Your friend is probably right. Like the Chinese government, create a limit on the time that a game is played. You and your friends can create a play schedule. That schedule should limit the playing to a window of time each day or every other day after school. Make a rule that no one is allowed to play outside of that time. Involving a guardian is a good idea. The guardian will help remind players when it's quitting time. He or she might also start offering rewards for being responsible players.

While playing like this will upset an addict, someone who loves gaming will welcome this. The gamer will be excited about the stable schedule. He or she will take care of other responsibilities before and after. Soon, a balance will be struck between loving the game and loving everything else.

An addict may complain and try to break the rules, so make up penalties for doing so. Someone who breaks the rules loses a whole day of game play. Addicts often say they'd rather have a little than nothing at all. The Chinese gaming addicts who were interviewed by the BBC said that without online gaming, their lives felt empty. An addict will bargain with a support group in order to keep gaming. Sometimes, this is just what's needed to get back to loving games for the sake of games.

Making Time for Important Things

If friends are not interested in the buddy system of scheduling, other things can be done. The goal is to gain control over the online gaming addiction. Addicts often feel powerless to their urges. They only feel good while gaming, and nothing else matters. Sometimes, they can't even help what they're doing. They just need to be gaming. This is further confused by the fact that games can be powerful.

The sense of winning or outsmarting the game or other players is powerful. The very thing that has control over the gamer is now making him or her feel powerful. This feeling of accomplishment can be addictive all by itself. It is our love of winning that makes us all strive to be better at things. Being a better gamer isn't bad—it's like wanting to be a better bowler or be better at math. It's just when the pursuit of getting better gets out of control that it becomes a problem.

A good way to start getting things under control for the lone gamer is to create a new schedule. The gamer starts with a list. This list should be everything that the gamer likes or liked to do before gaming became so important. The list should include all activities great and small. Activities such as spending time with a little brother or sister should be listed. Visiting with grandparents should be listed, too. Creating posters, drawing, playing basketball, cooking, and whatever is something that is fun to do—other than gaming—should be put on the list as well. If the list is short, the gamer can add things that he or she has always wanted to try but hasn't yet.

Each activity should be given a certain amount of time. These activities must come back into the gamer's life. They must get equal energy, enthusiasm, and attention. Assign at least one activity to a day, before and after gaming. Give gaming only a couple hours, if that. The gamer needs to allow gaming to take a backseat for awhile so that he or she can regain real power. Real power is being able to keep the gaming system off, even though it feels like there is nothing else to do. There is always something else to do, and many of these other things are just as fun and not as addictive.

Chapter five

WHEN HAS IT GONE TOO FAR?

Some gamers become so deeply involved in gaming that they reach out to like-minded groups. They join chat rooms and user groups so that they can talk about the game. They take as much pleasure in talking or thinking about the game as they do playing it. While chat rooms are a great way to meet friends, they are also dangerous. Chat rooms can be the "neighborhoods" where online predators stalk targets. Predators disguise themselves as teens or children. They talk like a gamer's friends would talk. They know exactly what to say to appear nonthreatening. A gamer's love for the game can be manipulated or controlled in a false way or for bad reasons.

Predators can simply tap into the gamer's love of gaming and start a friendship. If the gamer received a high score and posted it on a forum, predators can reply. They may congratulate the gamer and give him or her praise.

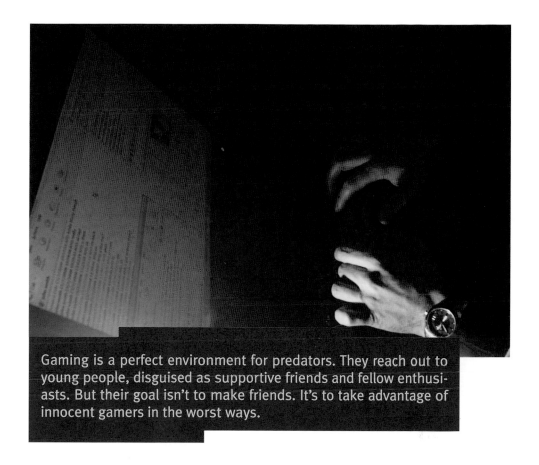

Gaming is a perfect environment for predators. They reach out to young people, disguised as supportive friends and fellow enthusiasts. But their goal isn't to make friends. It's to take advantage of innocent gamers in the worst ways.

They may ask for hints on how to beat the game. The gamer feels important and valued. Sometimes, we don't feel like that in real life. In chat rooms and on forums, it feels good because everyone else sees it, too. This is how predators work. They make a lonely gamer feel cared for or valuable. They may know other online users and make it seem like they're one big family. They may create other goals in the game that they and the gamer must accomplish. Soon, it seems like a bond has formed, and it's them against the world.

Gamers need to be extremely cautious about giving credit card and other financial information to any online source. Some companies are fake fronts for scams, some can overcharge fees or rack up hidden costs, and some are not hacker-safe.

Responses from other users like these can be innocent. Often, it may just be another gamer who is seeking friendship or conversation. It can really be just about the game, but many times it is not. A predator may be lurking and waiting for just the right moment to make things a little more private.

The moment a chat pal, forum member, subscriber, or player asks to contact someone in private, it should be a red flag. People say and do things in private that they cannot do in public. Predators want to have a private discussion so that they can manipulate the relationship even further. Gamers

Gaming addiction can lead to big debt. This online gamer, Greg Hogan, pleaded guilty to robbery. He is accused of robbing a bank in 2005 in order to pay off his online poker debts.

should never allow their addiction to the game to take them into private discussions with people they have met online. There are magazines, Web sites, fan sites, and fanzines that gamers can read and visit. The need to be private about gaming is not healthy.

The worst-case scenario ends with a gamer being attacked (mentally, physically, or sexually), kidnapped, or killed by someone that he or she has met online. It happens, which is why cyber friends need to be kept in the cyber realm. Anytime a chat room member or anyone else from the cyber world asks for personal information, gamers should log out. The person who asked for this information should be reported to the game's or Web site's owners immediately. Doing so makes the online gaming environment safer and better for everyone.

Money on the Game

While many online games are free, gaming systems and popular online games cost money. Individual games are relatively inexpensive. Subscriptions to online environments can become costly. No online purchases should be made without an adult. Not all sites are secure. Giving financial information over the Web is risky. Hackers are always looking for security weaknesses to steal credit card information. Once the information is stolen, it can be sold to identity thieves. These thieves make hundreds of purchases using other people's credit card numbers. This can cause financial problems and legal issues for card owners.

Some sites use games to make money off of the unsuspecting. They may request a small fee and then charge for things the gamer didn't want. Some sites offer subscriptions that seem cheap, but the cost compared to the playtime may be really expensive. Having a guardian approve of the site and purchase will save the gamer from unwanted trouble or dangerous purchases.

Gamers should never accept gifts from online friends, even though gaming is expensive. This is a bait that predators use. They buy gifts for youths who love playing but can't afford it. The predator's kindness is really just an attempt to get closer to the target: the gamer. Predators have even assured gamers that the gift is really because they both love the game. They may suggest visiting their place to get more games. There are far too many free games online to risk life and limb for a free game from an online "pal." A gamer should never agree to meet a cyber pal in person, free games or otherwise.

Addiction can often take a bite out of someone's budget. Drug addicts will steal and sell valuables for more drugs. Gamblers will bet their cars, houses, and large investments to try to "win big." Gamers may empty their piggy banks to pay for more games. They may take odd jobs around the neighborhood and blow their whole earning on games.

Everyone should have a little bit of money put aside. Rainy days, and the need for cash, always happen. Gamers should never leave themselves flat broke for games. For every game that is bought, $5 or $10 should be put aside for saving. If gamers don't have enough to buy the game and put a little

Gaming should never cause a financial pinch. The gaming world is full of free games; the gamer just has to look for them. Be wise about what is truly free and what isn't.

aside, they should wait until there is enough. Game addicts may try to make trades to get the games they want. Gamers should never agree to meet someone in private for a trade. A guardian must be involved, and the trade has to be in a public place. Anything less is taking too great a chance.

Online gamers may try to get versions of popular games for free that normally cost money. Sometimes, this is shareware. These types of files are created by programmers and are meant to be shared freely. In the gaming community, however, this isn't always the case. Downloads of "free" popular games can be traps. Once downloaded, they can ruin a computer, collect personal information for hackers, or cause glitches. Downloading plug-ins and upgrades for free is also dangerous. These should come from trusted sources. If the gamer isn't sure, he or she needs to ask an adult.

When Money Is the Draw

Games like *World of Warcraft* seem very real. They even have money and things to buy. The cyber money can be bought with real-world money (such as eight thousand pieces of gold for around $160). It gets even more crazy because in many games, points and cyber money can be exchanged for real-world goods. Earning gold or points may become just as addictive as playing the games. Gamers start to think that they are earning a living through their gaming. It's best to limit this type of gaming as much as possible. The real world is where the gamer should earn money. There will be enough time to work hard in order to

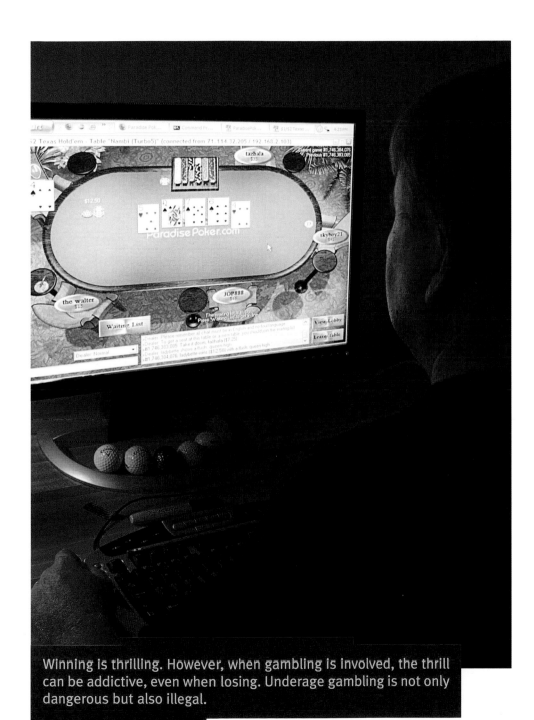

Winning is thrilling. However, when gambling is involved, the thrill can be addictive, even when losing. Underage gambling is not only dangerous but also illegal.

make a buck. Games should really be just about gaming and having fun.

Gambling

Many online games offer chances to win prizes through play. The makers of *World of Warcraft* have competitions with cash prizes. This is very different than a site that tells surfers that they can win big by paying a dollar or two. This is betting. The gamer is not buying the rights to play a game; he or she is betting on winning. Anything that says it's free, then asks for money, is to be avoided. Any site that promises big money with a small bet is something to quit, too. Online gaming addiction can very easily turn into online gambling addiction. This is where a gamer hopes to make money through gaming by placing money on the game.

Any person under the age of twenty-one who gambles online in the United States is breaking the law. While some adults do gamble online on sports and card games, the companies they use are not in the United States. Some lawmakers are hoping to make online gambling fully legal in the United States. Regardless, it will probably never be legal for kids to gamble. While addiction may be driving the need to gamble on a game, there are safe games where money is not at stake. The Federal Trade Commission warns that no child should ever give credit card information to gambling sites. The ease of betting can instantly create a huge bill. Before the gamer knows it, he or she is in debt for thousands of dollars. This can ruin a parent's or teen's credit history. One slight urge can lead to years of legal and financial woes.

The online community is full of great games. Educational Web sites offer games that are just as cool as popular shooting or action games. For every adventure, racing, or shooting game, a healthy gamer should also play a trivia game. This will allow him or her to have a lot of fun and escape a little but also grow as a person. Gamers seldom forget the interesting things they learn in games. This means that the mind loves to learn while having fun and have fun while learning. The best games give the gamer's mind both opportunities.

Glossary

accomplishment The completion of a task; an achievement.

addict A person who is mentally or physically dependent on something.

addictive Describes something that is capable of making a person mentally or physically dependent on it.

alter ego A second personality.

application A program or set of instructions that a computer follows to carry out certain activities.

avatar A changeable image that is used in computer gaming and computer applications to represent a person in the real world.

controversial Something that brings about debate.

dependent Needing to use, have, or experience something.

download To take a file or application from one source and copy it somewhere else (to another computer or disc).

etiquette The rules of how to behave toward others in a proper way.

fatigue Extreme tiredness.

interact To become involved with, communicate, or work with someone else.

Internet A network that links computers all over the world.

manipulate To control something or someone, usually in a false way or for bad reasons.

MMORPG Massively multiplayer online role-playing game; a game that allows hundreds of players to interact.

obese To be so overweight as to be at risk for several other diseases and life-threatening conditions.

physique A person's shape or body size.

privacy policy A set of rules that controls how personal information will be used.

regulations Official rules that state what may or may not be done.

social Relating to the way people in groups behave or interact.

syndrome A group of symptoms that make up a disease or condition.

terms of use The rules that state how something will be used, by the maker and the user.

withdraw To remove oneself from something or pull back from something.

Canadian Safety Council
1020 Thomas Spratt Place
Ottawa, ON K1G 5L5
Canada
(866) 658-9022
Web site: http://www.safety-council.org/info/
child/trojan.html
This is a Canadian national, not-for profit organization
that is dedicated to safety—including online safety.
The organization provides information on how to
stay safe online, as well as a hotline and contact Web
site to report problems. It also allows safe, anonymous reporting of online predators at: http://
www.cybertip.ca/app.en.

Connect for Kids
Forum for Youth Investment
7064 Eastern Avenue NW
Washington, DC 20012
(202) 207-3333
Web site: http://www.connectforkids.org
Connect for Kids is a Web site and resource center
that is operated by the Forum for Youth Investment, a
nonprofit that is dedicated to making sure that all young

people are ready for work, college, and life. The site has extensive resources about online gaming dangers and addictions.

Online Gamers Anonymous (OLGA/OLG-Anon)
P.O. Box 3433
Brentwood, TN 37024
(612) 245-1115
Web site: http://www.olganon.org
This is a not-for-profit organization that "provides a resource for open discussion, support, education, and referrals." Like other addiction programs, it supports a twelve-step recovery program.

Teenage Gambling Addiction
Nathan Hale Drive, Suite 840
Coventry, CT 06238
Web site: http://www.teenage-gambling-addiction.org
This is a Web portal that offers advice on how to help a teenage gambler. The site offers testimonials and links to books for purchase. It also manages an online chat room about teen gambling addiction, whether it be online or offline gambling.

WiredKids.org
96 Linwood Plaza, #417
Fort Lee, NJ 07024-3701
Web site: http://www.wiredkids.org

For teens: http://www.wiredkids.org/teens/index.html
Wired Kids, Inc., is an organization that is dedicated to the online safety of kids, teens, and families. Wired Safety is the "world's largest Internet safety, help, and education resource."

Web Sites

Due to the changing nature of Internet links, Rosen Publishing has developed an online list of Web sites related to the subject of this book. This site is updated regularly. Please use this link to access the list:

http://www.rosenlinks.com/faq/onga

For Further Reading

Criddle, Linda. *Look Both Ways: Help Protect Your Family on the Internet.* Redmond, WA: Microsoft Press, 2006.

Fisanick, Christina. *Addiction.* Farmington Hills, MI: Gale Group, 2009.

Kern, Jan. *Eyes Online, Eyes on Life: A Journey Out of Online Addictions.* Cincinnati, OH: Standard Publishing, 2008.

Rothman, Kevin F. *Coping with Dangers on the Internet.* New York, NY: Rosen Publishing Group, 2000.

Schaefer, Wyatt, ed. *Addiction.* Farmington Hills, MI: Cengage Gale, 2007.

Sommers, Michael A. *The Dangers of Online Predators.* New York, NY: Rosen Publishing, 2008.

Stoehr, James D. *The Neurobiology of Addiction.* New York, NY: Facts On File, Inc., 2005.

Thakkar, Vastal. *Addiction.* New York, NY: Chelsea House Publishers, 2006.

Willard, Nancy E. *Cyber-Safe Kids, Cyber Savvy Teens: Helping Young People Learn to Use the Internet Safely and Responsibly.* San Francisco, CA: John Wiley & Sons, Inc., 2007.

Index

About the Author

Holly Cefrey is an award-winning children's book author. While she grew up in the age of early home gaming systems, she has become an online trivia game enthusiast in her adult life. She enjoys the online world, with an understanding of how addictive it can be without moderation. Her favorite games are from museum-based educational Web sites. She has also designed Web sites and Web graphics.

Photo Credits

Cover © www.istockphoto.com/VM; pp. 6, 27, 40 Shutterstock.com; p. 9 Dan McCoy/Time & Life Pictures/Getty Images; pp. 10, 36–37, 48 © AP Images; 14 © The Orange County Register/Zuma Press; p. 16 © www.istockphoto.com/Dawn Liljenquist; p. 18 © www.istockphoto.com/Bonnie Jacobs; p. 25 © www.istockphoto.com/Alberto Pomares; p. 28 © www.istockphoto.com/Lisa F. Young; p. 38 © www.istockphoto.com/Tomaz Levstek; p. 45 Joe Raedle/Getty Images; pp. 46–47 © www.istockphoto.com/David Freund; p. 51 © www.istockphoto.com/George M. Muresan; p. 53 Karen Bleier/AFP/Getty Images.

Designer: Nicole Russo; Editor: Nicholas Croce; Photo Researcher: Cindy Reiman